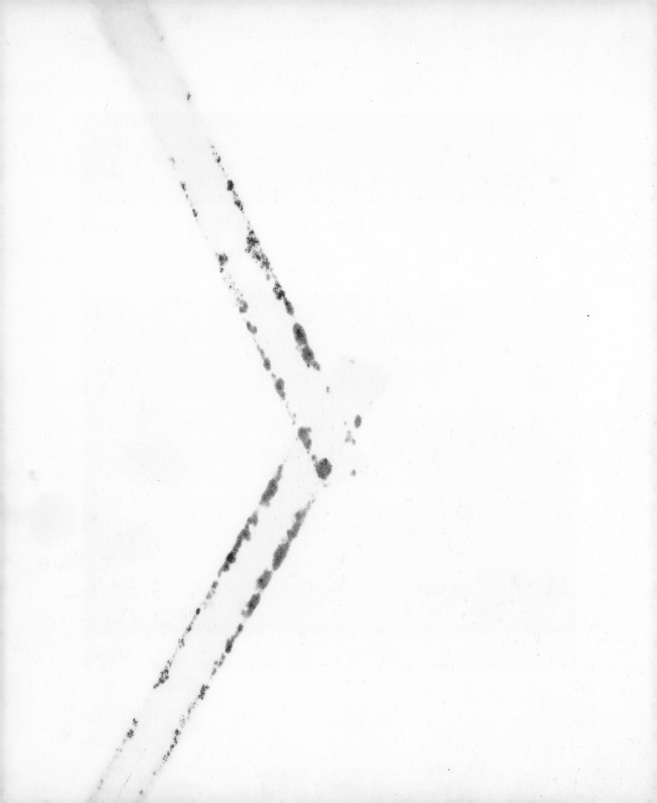

SCIENCE PUZZLES

Laurence B. White, Jr.

drawings by

Marc Tolon Brown

Addison-Wesley

Books by Laurence B. White, Jr.

Science Games
Science Puzzles
Science Toys
Science Tricks
Investigating Science with Coins
Investigating Science with Nails
Investigating Science with Paper
Investigating Science with Rubber Bands
So You Want to be a Magician?

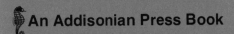 **An Addisonian Press Book**

To Dave . . .
who guarantees every experiment
because they worked for him

Text Copyright ©1975 by Laurence B. White, Jr.
Illustrations Copyright ©1975 by Marc Tolon Brown
All Rights Reserved
Addison-Wesley Publishing Company, Inc.
Reading, Massachusetts 01867
Printed in the United States of America
First Printing

HA/WZ   08602   3/75

Library of Congress Cataloging in Publication Data

White, Laurence B
  Science puzzles.

  SUMMARY: These simple science puzzles and experiments include experiments with mirrors, footprints, ice
cubes, soup cans, and water."
  "An Addisonian Press book."
  1. Science—Experiments—Juvenile literature.
[1. Science—Experiments] I. Brown, Marc Tolon, illus.
II. Title.
Q163.W4885   507'.2   74–2155
ISBN 0–201–08602–6

Puzzles are to Think

A puzzle is a puzzle. . .

. . .only until you know the answer!

A science investigation is a puzzle, too. . .

. . .until you understand it!

This is a book of science puzzles.

Can you. . .

- Freeze a penny in the middle of an ice cube?
- Turn yourself upside down with a teaspoon?
- Eat an apple without tasting it?

Learn the answers. . .

Start investigating!

Can You Count to Twenty?

Watch a friend (maybe a teacher).
Do not tell him what you are doing.
Watch him blink.
Start counting slowly.
One, two, three, four, five . . .
Can you reach 20 before he blinks again?
No! We are always blinking our eyes.
Try to count to 20 and not blink yourself.
Can you do it?

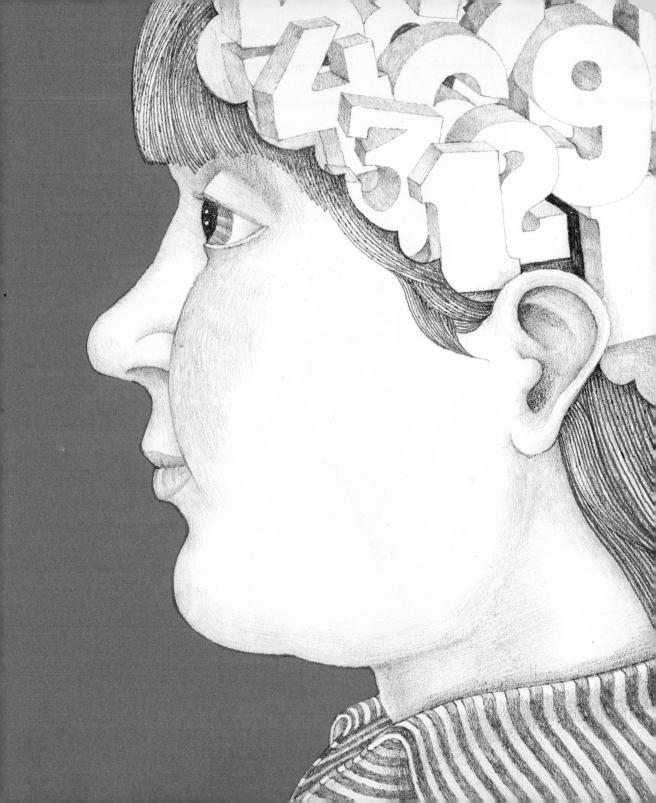

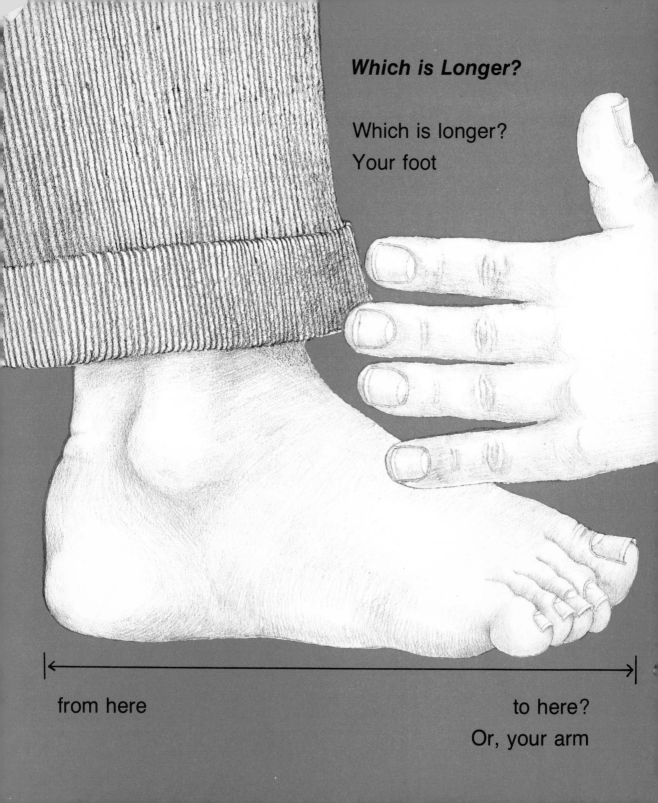

Which is Longer?

Which is longer?
Your foot

from here

to here?

Or, your arm

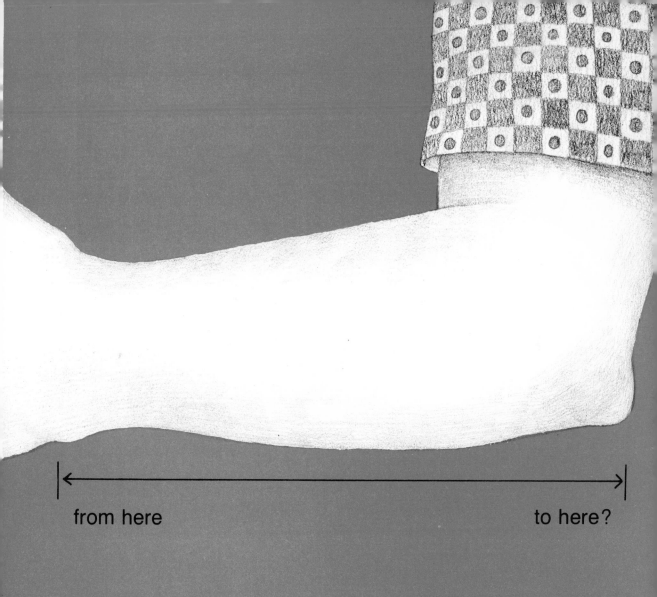

from here   to here?

It is not your arm.

It is not your foot.

They are both about the same length.

Prove it!

Measure them.

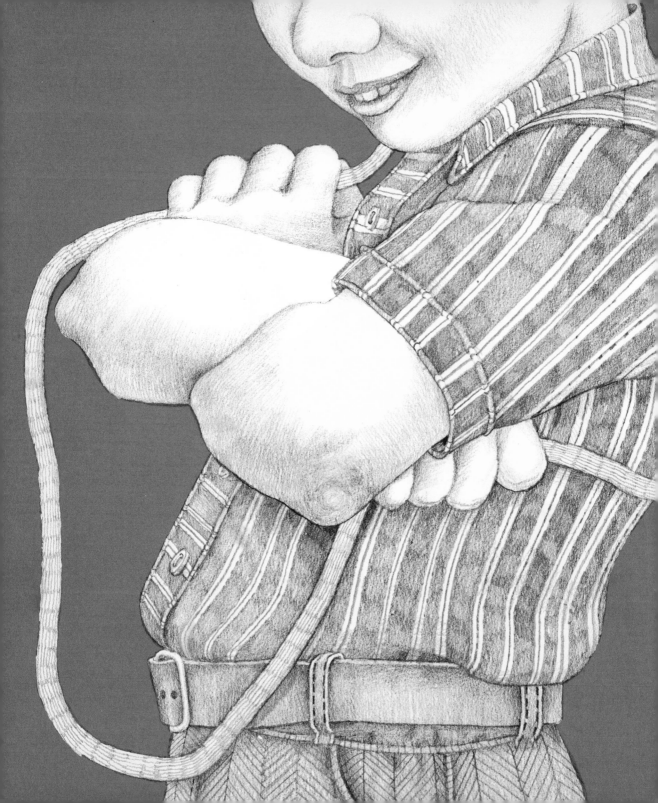

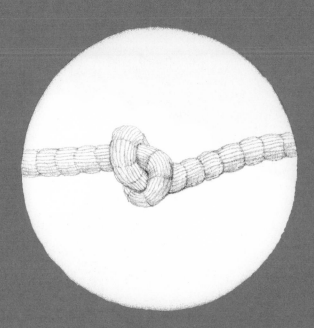

What Happens When You Open Your Arms?

Cross your arms like this.

Hold the ends of a rope tightly in each hand.

Open your arms.

What happens to the rope?

It is tied in a knot.

Why?

You had your arms in a knot.

The knot went over to the rope.

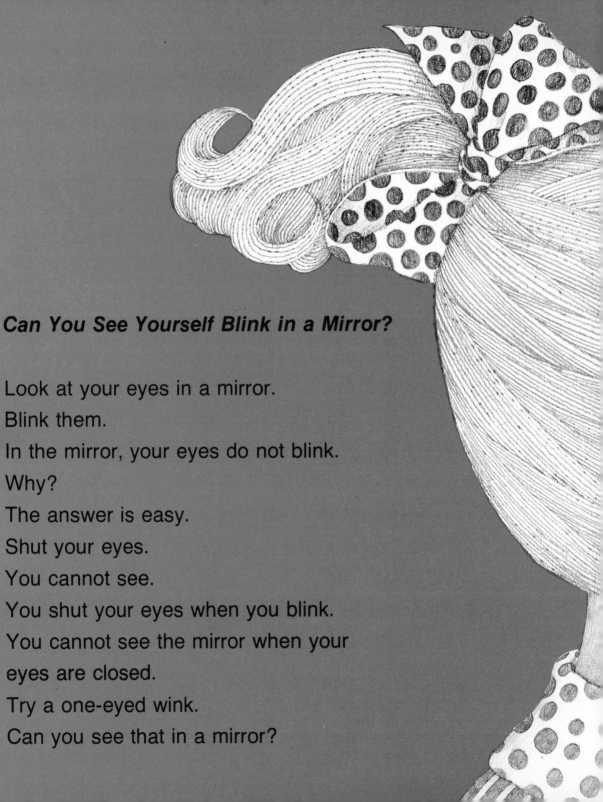

Can You See Yourself Blink in a Mirror?

Look at your eyes in a mirror.
Blink them.
In the mirror, your eyes do not blink.
Why?
The answer is easy.
Shut your eyes.
You cannot see.
You shut your eyes when you blink.
You cannot see the mirror when your
eyes are closed.
Try a one-eyed wink.
Can you see that in a mirror?

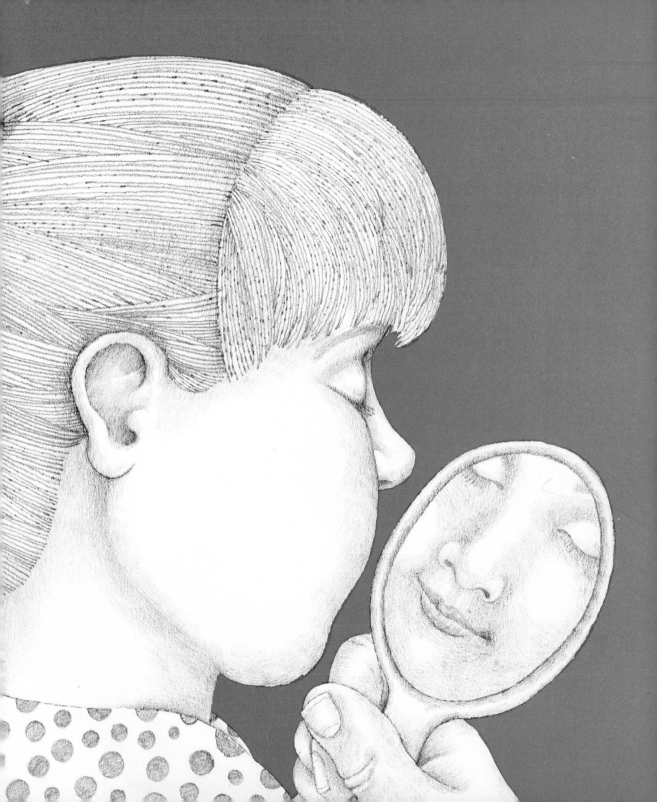

Turn Yourself Upside Down

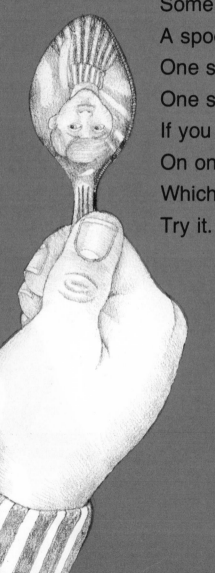

Look into a mirror.
You see yourself right side up.
Some mirrors turn things upside down.
A spoon is a mirror.
One side curves in.
One side curves out.
If you look at a spoon, you will see yourself.
On one side you will be upside down.
Which side?
Try it.

What Does This Say?

Hold this word to a mirror.

ƎVAD

The mirror turns the word around.
You can write like this.
Print a word on a thin paper.
Turn it over and hold it up to a window.
Copy the letters through the paper.
This is your backwards word.
You can only read it in a mirror.

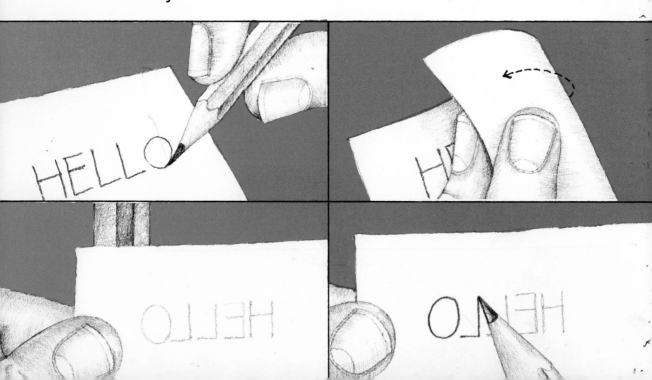

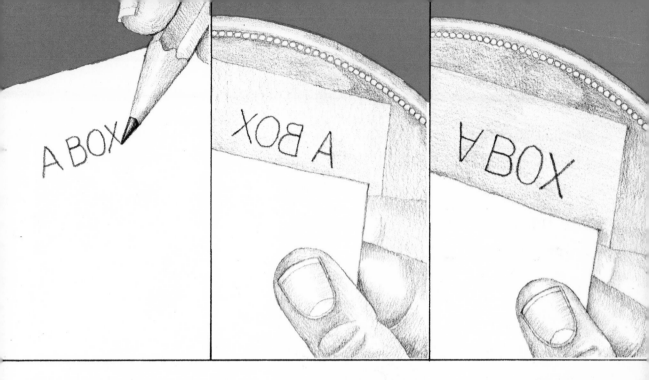

Can a Mirror Fool You?

Print "A BOX" on a piece of paper.

Look at it in a mirror.

While you are looking, turn it upside down.

Look!

"A" is upside down.

But "BOX" is not.

Why?

The letters "B O X" look the same upside down.

The letter "A" looks different upside down.

The Bright School
Chattanooga, Tennessee

Whose Footprints are These?

Which set of footprints was made by a person?
They are both people's footprints.

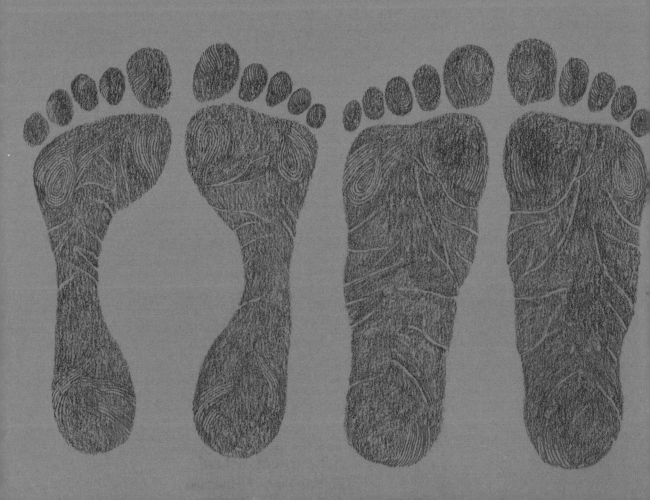

Most people's footprints look like these.
Here the insides of the feet do not touch the floor.

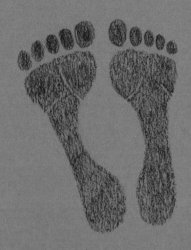

But this person has flat feet.

When you take a bath,
Step on the floor with wet feet.
Which set of footprints do you have?
(Be sure to wipe them up!)

Which Hand Feels Colder?

Next time you wash your hands, try this.

Dip both hands in the water.

Hold both hands up.

Which hand feels colder?

They are both the same.

Can you make one colder?

Blow on it.

Wind dries the water.

When the water dries, it makes you cold!

Can You Make Paper Fall Faster?

Hold two sheets of flat paper side by side.
Let them fall together.
Air makes them fall slowly.
Can you make one fall faster?
Roll one sheet into a ball.
Drop the ball and the flat sheet.
The ball drops faster.
The air does not slow it down.

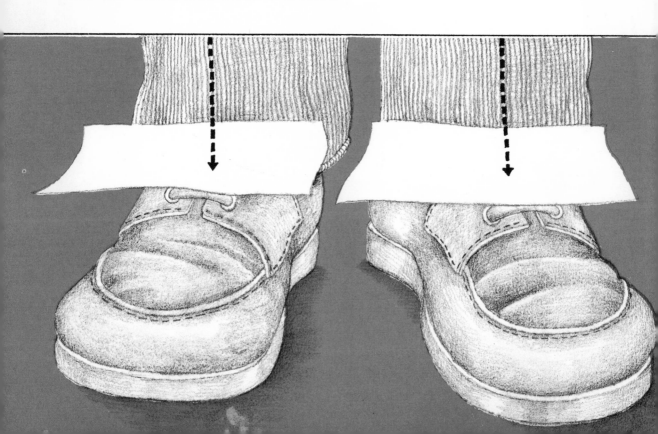

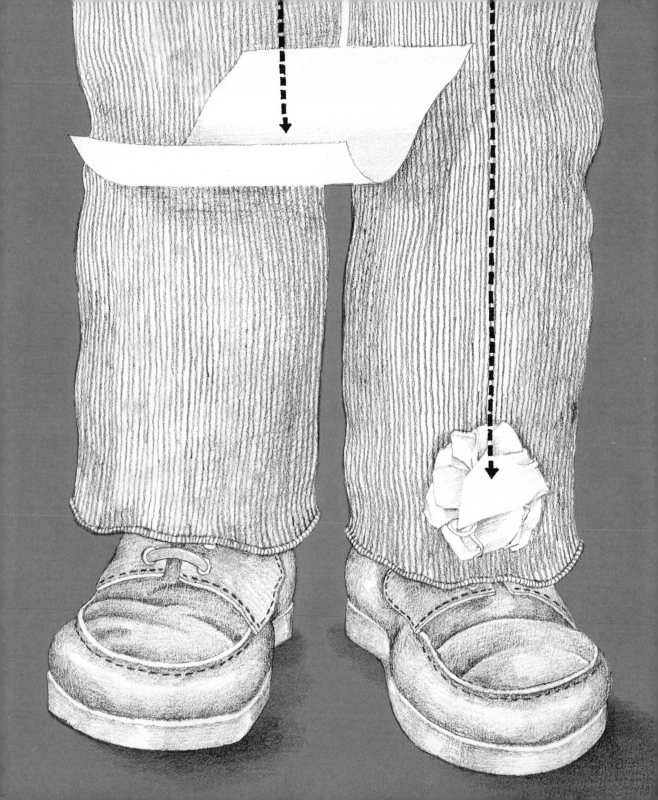

Can You Hear with Your Teeth?

Scratch a pencil with your fingernail.
Can you hear the scratching?
You can hear it just a little.
Hold the pencil in your teeth.
Scratch it.
The scratching noise will be louder.
The noise goes through your teeth,
through your skull,
right to your ears!

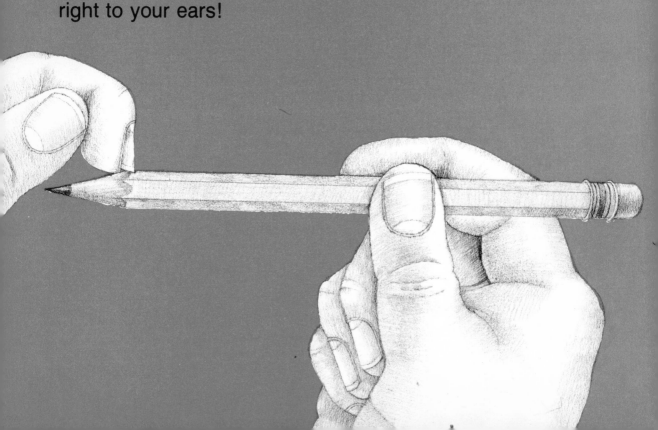

What Holds the Pencil Up?

This looks like a magic trick.
The pencil is not really stuck on the hands.
What holds it up?
Look very carefully.
Most people do not look sharply enough.
Did you?
(Count the number of fingers).

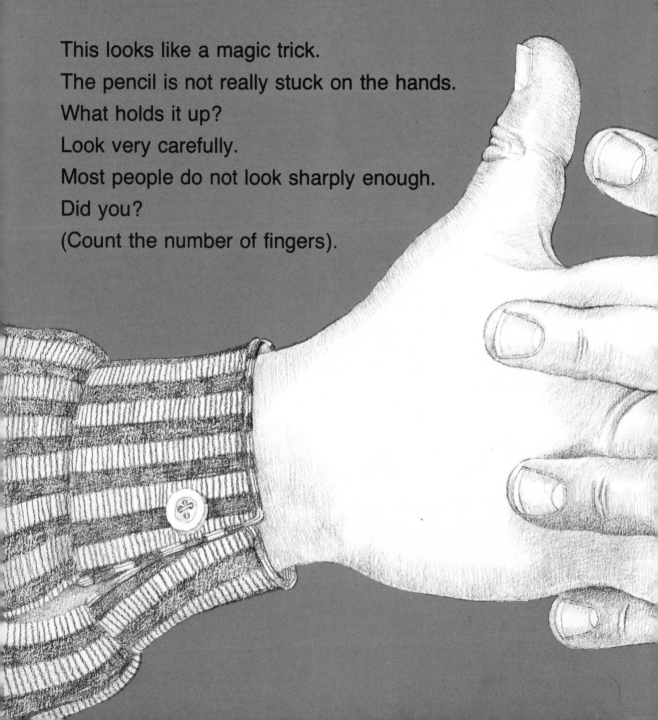

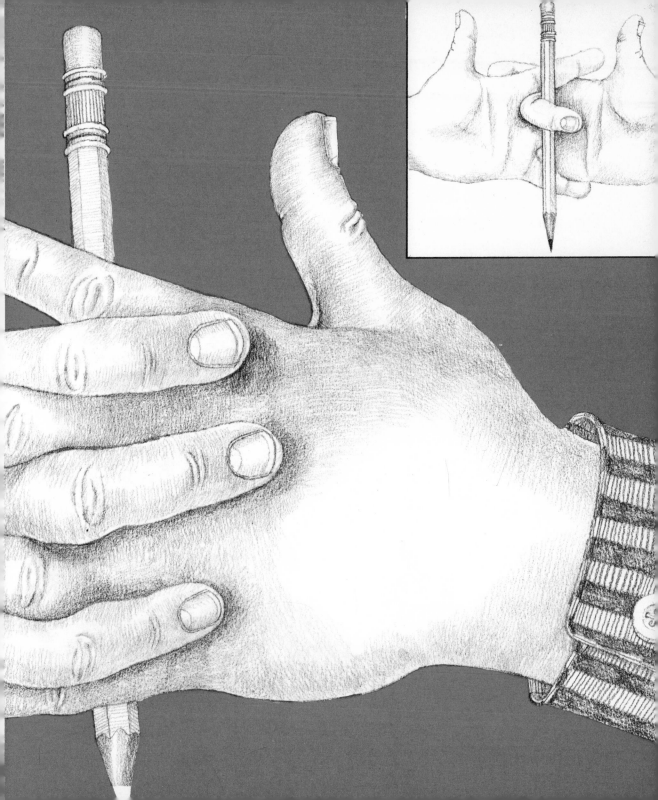

Can You Blow a Square Bubble?

Are soap bubbles always round?
Get a piece of wire. (A paper clip will work).
Bend it square, with a little handle.
Dip it in some dishwashing liquid.
Blow into it.
Make a bubble.
Surprise!
The bubble is round!

Can You Make an Ice Cube with a Penny Inside?

Puzzle your friends with the ice cube.

It has a penny frozen inside.

How?

Fill a paper cup half full of water.

Set it in a freezer until it is frozen.

Put a penny on top of the ice.

Pour some water on top.

Freeze it again.

Tear the cup away from the ice.

The penny is in the ice cube!

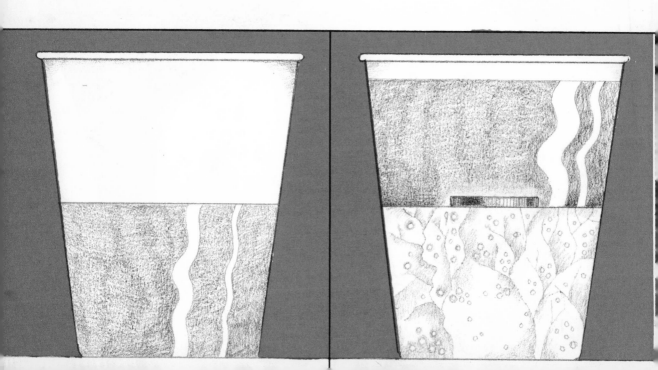

Which Hole Squirts Best?

Do this puzzle over a sink.

Punch three holes in a paper cup.

Use a pencil point.

Fill the cup with water.

The water squirts out the holes.

Which hole squirts best?

The bottom hole squirts best.

The water is deeper.

The deeper water pushes out harder.

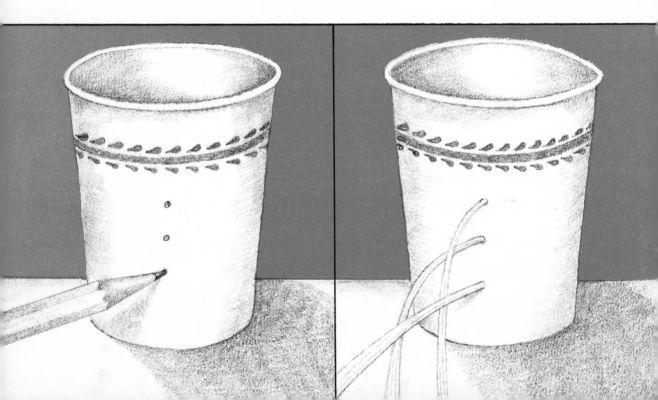

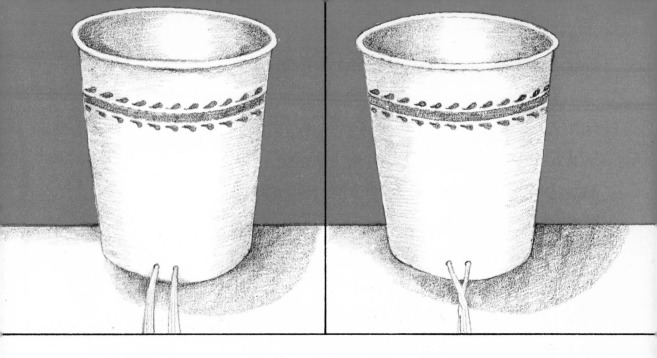

Will Water Stick to Itself?

Poke two small holes in a paper cup.

Make them close together, near the bottom.

Fill the cup with water over a sink.

Two little streams squirt out.

Pinch the two streams together with your fingers.

The two streams stick together!

Break them apart with your fingers.

Pinch them together again.

Water sticks to itself.

Can You Push a Straw Into an Apple?

Put an apple on the table.
Hold a paper drinking straw by one end.
Try to push the other end into the apple.
You cannot.
The apple seems too tough.
But hold a straw above the apple.
Push it down fast.Now the straw is moving quickly.
It does not stop.
It goes right into the apple.

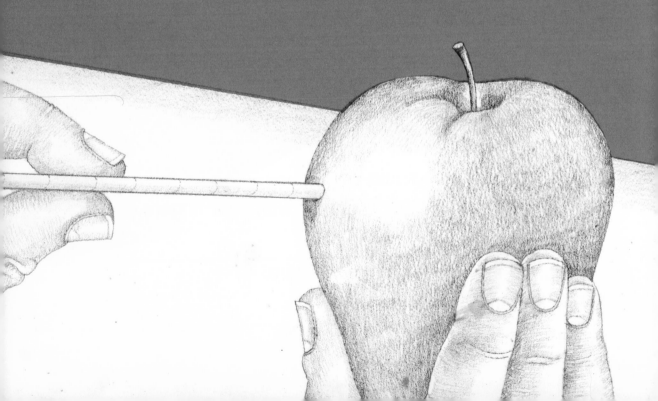

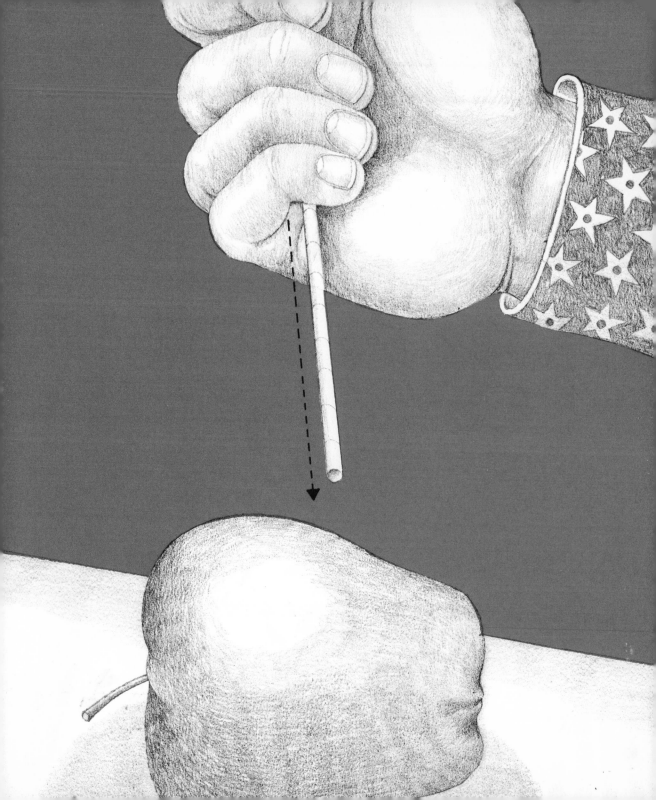

Will They Sink or Float?

Fill a bowl with water.

Drop a raw carrot and an apple into the water.

One will sink.

One will float.

Will the apple float or sink?

Things heavier than water sink.

Things lighter than water float.

The carrot is heavier than water.

Does Your Nose Help You Taste Food?

Get an apple and a potato.
Cut some small pieces of each.
Put them in a paper bag.
Reach in and take a piece out.
Do not look at it.
Hold your nose tightly.
Eat the piece.
Is it an apple or a potato?
You cannot tell.
You cannot taste it.
Your nose does help you taste food.

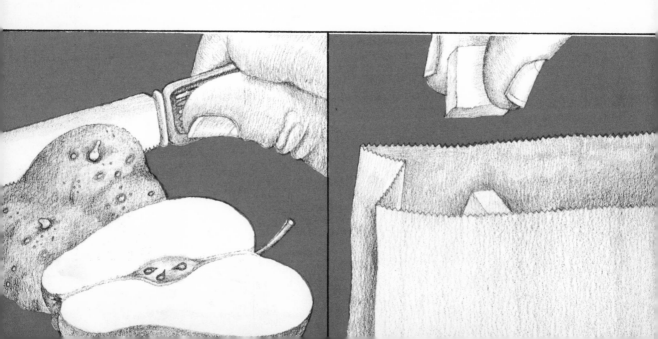

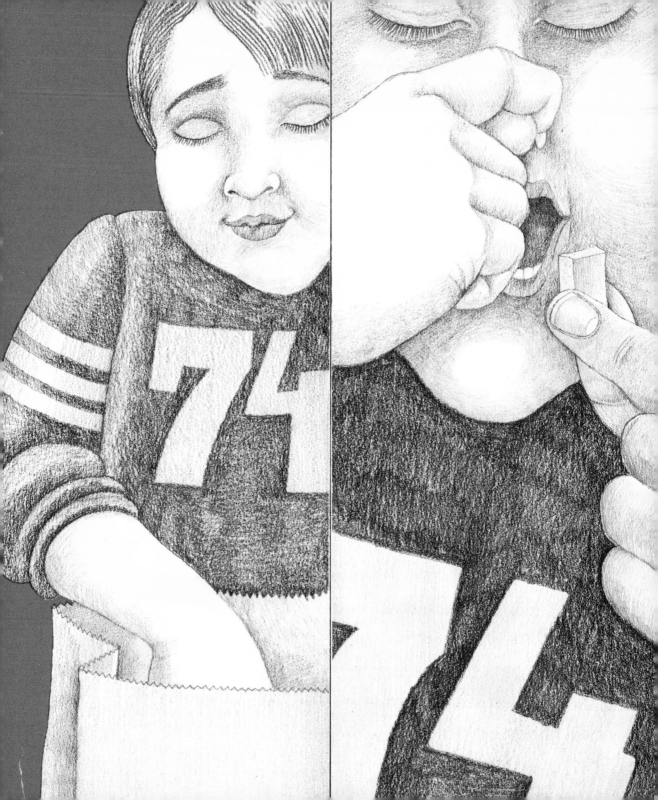

Can You Take Salt and Pepper Apart?

Sprinkle some salt and pepper in an empty paper cup.

Shake the cup to mix them together.

Can you take them apart again?

Pour some water in the cup.

The pepper floats on top.

The salt stays on the bottom.

Salt is heavier than pepper.

Can You Mix These?

Pour a little cooking oil in a clear glass.
Pour in some water.
See what happens?
The water goes down.
The oil floats on top.
Can you mix them together?
Try with a spoon.
After you stir them, wait a minute.
They go apart again.
Some things do not mix.

What Makes a Rainbow?

Do this outdoors in bright sunlight.
Set a clear glass on a piece of white paper.
Fill the glass half full of water.
Tip the glass back and forth.
Look on the paper.
You will see spots of pretty colors.
Sometimes the sun shines on tiny water drops in the sky.
The light turns red, orange, yellow, green, blue and purple.
It is a rainbow!
Your glass makes rainbow colors the same way.

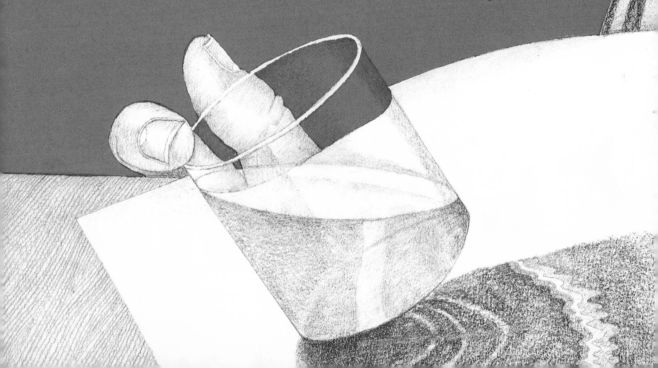

Can You Blow a Book Over?

Set two heavy books close together on a table.
They should stand on their ends.
Can you blow either one over?
No?
You can when you know the trick.
Blow up a balloon between them.
Your breath fills the balloon.
A book falls over.

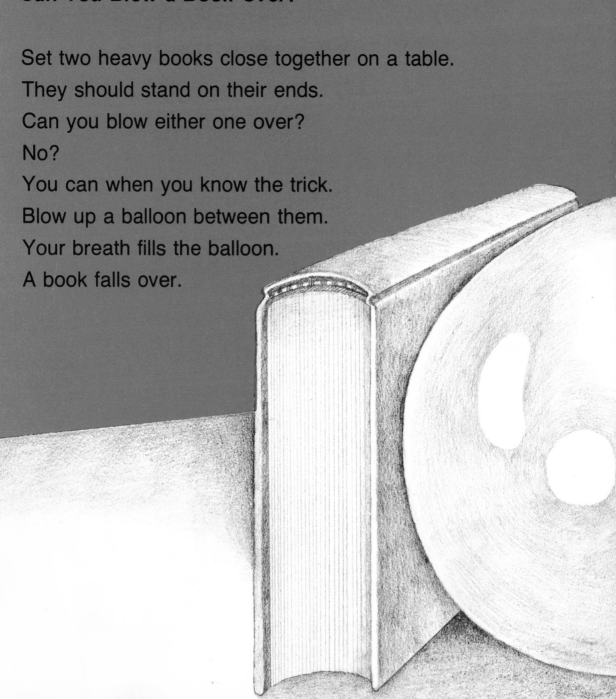

Which Can Will Win?

Take two soup cans, one empty one and one filled with soup.

Race them side by side down a hill.

One will always win.

Which one?

The full one!

It is heavier.

It goes faster.

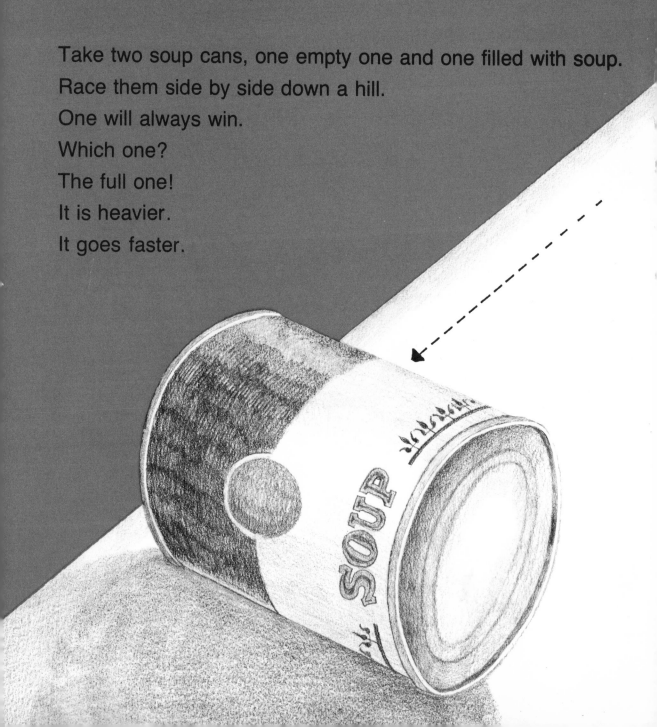

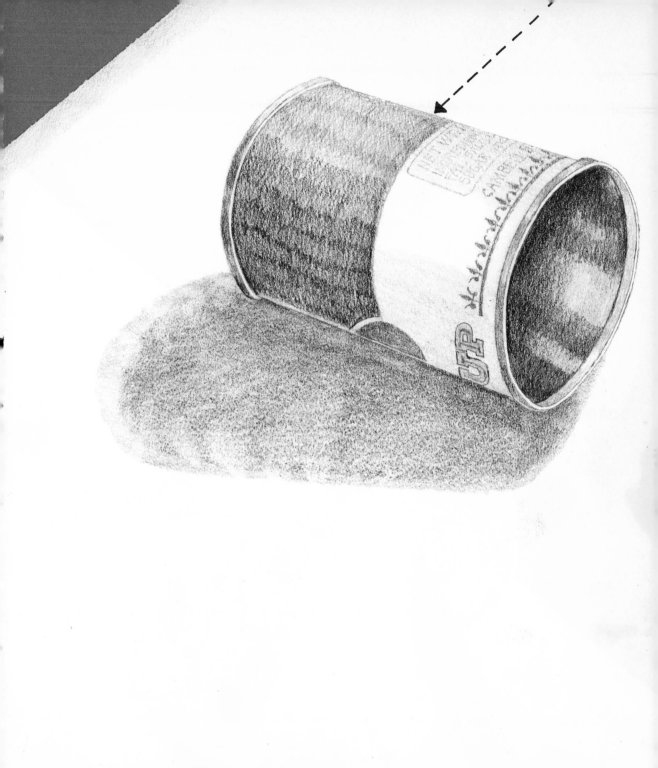

Which Nail Makes the Highest Note?

Nails can make pretty music.

Tie some on a piece of string.

Use different sizes of nails.

Hold the end of the string in your hand.

Tap the nails with another nail.

Each one makes a different musical note.

Do little nails make high or low notes?

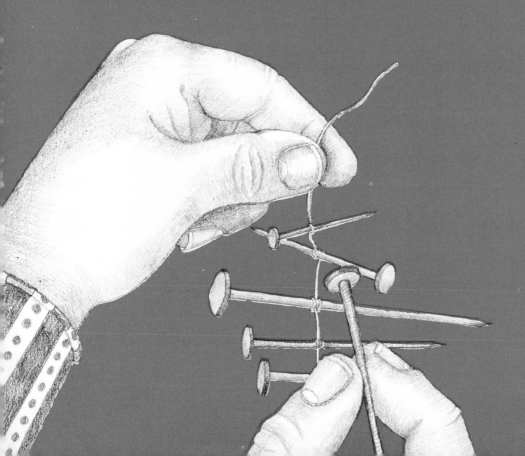

These puzzles are not puzzles any more.
You know the answers.
What can you do now?
Find some science puzzles of your own.
Look around.
Ask questions.
Try things.
Anything you do not understand is just a puzzle
looking for an answer.

DATE DUE

Hodge					
Henson					
Blair					